50
DATES
WORSE
THAN
YOURS

50
DATES

WORSE
THAN
YOURS

Justin Racz

BLOOMSBURY

Published by Bloomsbury USA, New York
Distributed to the trade by Holtzbrinck Publishers

All papers used by Bloomsbury USA are natural, recyclable products made from wood
grown in well-managed forests. The manufacturing processes conform to the environmental
regulations of the country of origin.

Library of Congress Cataloging-in-Publication Data has been applied for.

ISBN 1-59691-264-2
ISBN-13 978-1-59691-264-9

First U.S. Edition 2007

1 3 5 7 9 10 8 6 4 2

Designed by Elizabeth Van Itallie and Justin Racz
Printed in Singapore by Tien Wah Press

For Julie.

Thank you for taking me away from the madness.

Contents

1. Proposes on First Date

THE DATE

Terminally ill or in serious need of a tax break, he pops the question.

LOCATION

His living room, next to the Xbox. Certainly not the romantic, twilit streets of Paris that you had dreamed of telling your children about one day.

HE SAID

"I'm a gambling man by nature . . . so deal or no deal?"

SHE SAID

"What's your name again?"

BEST PART

At least he's not afraid of commitment.

WORST PART

You actually considered it for a minute.

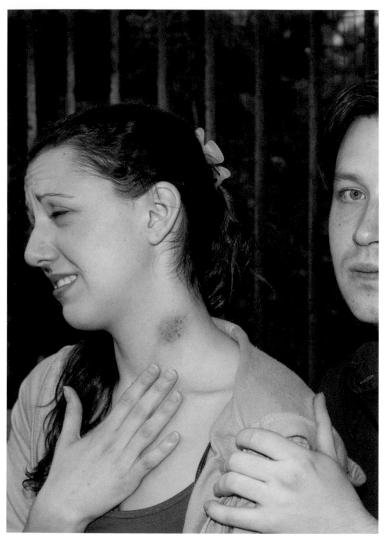

2. Joe Hickey

THE DATE

Things were actually going well—until, when it was time for the kiss, he pushed your face to the side and clamped onto your neck.

DRESS

That night it was boatneck shirt. The next day, turtleneck.

HE SAID

"You taste delicious."

SHE SAID

"You're hurting my trachea."

BEST PART

At least he didn't have braces (see date number 16).

WORST PART

Having everyone in your office know you just got a hickey because, really, who wears a turtleneck in July?

3. The Doodler

THE DATE

You know it's going poorly when your date takes out a ballpoint pen and starts doodling like a sixth grader bored out of her mind in social studies class.

LOCATION

Kiddie Burgers and Buns—paper tablecloths and markers provided.

HE SAID

"I've heard art therapy can be really helpful."

SHE SAID

"Huh? Whah? Sorry, I think I finally figured out how to win tic-tac-toe every time."

BEST PART

When she goes to the bathroom, you break her pen.

WORST PART

She starts playing hangman, with an alarmingly lifelike portrait of your head in a noose.

4. Karaoke

THE DATE

Once they were both well-lubricated with gin and tonics, they found their way in front of a sweaty microphone, singing hits from the '70s and '80s. Poorly.

LOCATION

Wong's Sing Sing on amateur night.

HE SANG

"I Want Your Sex" and "Feel Like Making Love."

SHE SANG

"I Will Survive"—right before collapsing in her own vomit.

BEST PART

She blacked out most of the night. The next day, he reminded her of her performance by e-mailing the video he recorded with his cell phone.

WORST PART

He, and his dry cleaner, will never forget.

5. She Was in It for the Meal

THE DATE

She showed up late and made more eye contact with the kobe beef burger than with you.

DRESS

No idea. It was difficult noticing anything as she vacuumed up the dessert-for-two platter.

HE SAID

"Um, I wasn't finished with that yet."

SHE SAID

"Can I have a doggy bag?"

BEST PART

Given the $250 tab, you'll definitely get a good table next time.

WORST PART

The $250 tab.

6. Surprise! You Were Related!

THE DATE

After making out, it's back to her place where she starts flipping through the family album. Hmm, her cousin Jeffrey looks an awful lot like your cousin Jeffrey.

THE COST

Six years of therapy.

HE SAID

"Well, the wedding would be half the size."

SHE SAID

"What happens in the family, stays in the family, you dig?"

BEST PART

Move to Utah, join a compound, and it's all good.

WORST PART

You liked it.

7. Shorter in Person

THE DATE

In his online photo he must be standing on a milk crate, or is in midair after jumping on a trampoline.

DRESS

OshKosh B'Gosh from the boys' section of the local department store.

HE SAID

(*in a deep baritone voice*) "Yeah, I know, I slouch."

SHE SAID

(*to the waiter*) "I'll have the grilled shrimp. Oops, sorry."

BEST PART

It's very easy to look over his head and scan the room for other possibilities.

WORST PART

When the waiter handed him the children's menu.

8. Painfully Chivalrous

THE DATE

He arrived at your place early, brought a bouquet, opened the car door for you, and fastened your seat belt. At the restaurant he pulled the seat out for you, ordered for you, and fed you. After he drove you home, he walked you to the door and asked if you'd like him to go inside and turn on the lights. At his insistence, you called him when you got to your bedroom safely.

DRESS

Bow tie.

HE SAID

"May I kiss you? Can I put my hand here?"

SHE SAID

"Can I gag you?"

BEST PART

Bringing him to your women's studies class for show and tell.

WORST PART

He wasn't so gracious when the bill came.

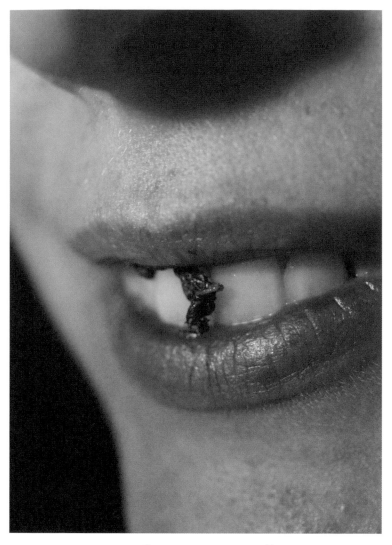

9. Spinach in Teeth

THE DATE

Fantastic! It couldn't have gone better. That is, until you looked in the mirror when you got home.

LOCATION

Lodged between two front teeth.

HE SAID

Nothing, the jerk.

SHE SAID

(*Later to her friend*) "I now regret telling him his fly was open."

BEST PART

The incident has encouraged active flossing between courses.

WORST PART

You can never really let go of the idea that he might have been "the one."

10. Ménage à Blackberry

THE DATE

It's just you, your date, and your handheld devices.

MEAL

Largely untouched. Who has the time?

HE SAID

"Sorry, it's Singapore. I have to take this."

SHE SAID

"Is that the new Treo 8700C with Quad Band? That's hot."

BEST PART

You both share the same backward priorities: work before sex . . . and work again right after sex.

WORST PART

She's more stimulated by the repeated vibrating e-mail notifications than you.

11. Hope You Like Meat

THE DATE

All you can eat $9.95 prime rib, ham off the bone, and every kind of wiener and wurst you've ever seen.

DRESS

Bib optional, but recommended.

HE SAID

"Pace yourself. The dessert bar is killer."

SHE SAID

"No, I will not 'take this napkin and wrap up those spare ribs and put them in my purse' for you."

BEST PART

You can always eat through the awkward silence.

WORST PART

The trichinosis.

12. Conjugal Visit

THE DATE

Long-distance relationships are always a trial. It only gets worse when the law is involved.

LOCATION

A classy cell specifically designed for the purpose. Hopefully they change the sheets, if there are any.

HE SAID

"Honey, I've only got ten minutes. Let's make the most of it."

SHE SAID

"Wait. I really want to talk first."

BEST PART

Warden says he's a model inmate and with continued good behavior he could get released on the low side of his three-to-five-year stretch.

WORST PART

That's not exactly something a girl can boast about to her parents and friends.

13. Peep Show

THE DATE

When he invited you to a "private screening," this wasn't exactly what you had in mind.

COST

Twenty-five cents for three minutes. Don't worry, he brought rolls of quarters.

HE SAID

"Take away nudity and the three-ways and it's a lot like *Phantom*."

SHE SAID

"If you ever talk to me again I'm calling the police."

BEST PART

When his quarters ran out.

WORST PART

It looked like he still had a roll in his pocket when he got up to leave.

14. Passover

THE DATE

The holiday requires Jews to open their doors to all those who do not have a place to go to celebrate Passover. All his older brothers and sisters are married, so you better look good.

 LOCATION

Grandma Bubbe's stuffy one-bedroom apartment in Queens.

 HE SAID

"Why is this night different from all other nights? Because you look Jewlicious."

 SHE SAID

"Why is your grandmother crying?"

 BEST PART

When he preemptively called you his girlfriend and kissed you on the cheek.

 WORST PART

His gefilte fish breath.

15. Vegas "Date"

THE DATE

She accidentally "ran into" him at the $25 progressive blackjack table. He turned $100 into $500—which later ended up in her purse.

LOCATION

Room 1123 at the Bellagio.

HE SAID

"Wow! We have real chemistry."

SHE SAID

"That will be $1,000."

BEST PART

She threw in a lap dance.

WORST PART

And a rash.

16. First Date

THE DATE

Dad drove them to the mall where they walked around for three hours, bought Pepsis, and killed time before they had to go into the dreaded photo booth. Would he make a move? The pressure was on. He'd told his friends that he would totally get to first base. His friends demanded proof.

COST

Two weeks allowance. Fifteen years of self-confidence.

HE SAID

(*To himself*) "I hope locking braces is an urban legend."

SHE SAID

(*To herself*) "I hope, like, all this time spent practicing kissing my pillow pays off."

BEST PART

Thirty years later, both divorced, they met up at their twentieth high school reunion. He had the old photo strip in his wallet and took it out. They married a year later.

WORST PART

He's still a lousy kisser.

17. Too Hot

THE DATE

You can't take your eyes off her. And neither can any guy in the restaurant.

LOCATION

Not the Olive Garden. The only olives she eats come directly off the olive trees of millionaires' third homes in Tuscany.

HE SAID

Nothing memorable.

SHE SAID

Whatever she wants.

BEST PART

For a moment, you actually think you have a shot. You believe those fortune cookies that told you personality and a sense of humor will take you far.

WORST PART

Being pushed out of the way by the paparazzi. Returning from the restroom to find another man in your seat.

18. Dating the Bartender

THE DATE

You finally got the courage to ask your local bartender on a date. Of course, you thought that meant something besides watching him work all night as he attempts to catch liquor bottles behind his back Tom Cruise style.

LOCATION

Stool.

HE SAID

"I'll be with you in a minute."

SHE SAID

"My name is *Cindy*. Not Suzie."

BEST PART

He's great looking. Bartenders can't live off tips and be ugly at the same time.

WORST PART

He is also on a date with the girl playing pool. And the one outside having a cigarette.

19. AA Meeting

THE DATE

Sitting close to each other on folding chairs in a church basement, you can't help but develop feelings for each other.

COST

$0. Even the coffee and sugar cookies are free.

HE SAID

"My name is Steve, and I'm an alcoholic."

SHE SAID

"My name is Doris, and *I'm* an alcoholic, too!"

BEST PART

It's cute when he text messages you during the meeting.

WORST PART

Your sponsors sit between you.

20. Kiddy Date

THE DATE

What is this, a playdate? (See date number 40.) What are you guys, nine? By age twenty-three, the motorized duck has lost some of its novelty.

LOCATION

Bert's Puppet and S'more House.

HE SAID

"I think it's really important to stay in touch with your inner child."

SHE SAID

"Please don't make me give you another piggyback ride."

BEST PART

Chicken fingers and french fries are good no matter what age you are.

WORST PART

When he tries to kiss her, all the nine-year-olds circle around, singing "FIRST COMES LOVE, THEN COMES MARRIAGE, THEN COMES A BABY IN THE BABY CAR-RIAGE!" It was embarrassing in elementary school; it's still painful.

21. Protest Rally

THE DATE

That passionate Che Guevara wannabe finally asked you out.

COST

Cardboard, markers—on him.

HE SAID

(*As he straps on a gas mask*) "Better safe than sorry."

SHE SAID

"How do you spell 'Condoleezza?'"

BEST PART

He wants to see you again—in D.C. for the Million Man March. It must be getting serious.

WORST PART

The one-hour wait for the porta-potty. And once you're in? No t.p.

22. *Almost* Divorced

THE DATE

Actually, he's just separated. He hasn't moved out, but he's filing for divorce. It's just a matter of time until it's official. Honest.

LOCATION

Dinner, a few towns away.

HE SAID

(*As he takes her hand*) "I can't tell you how wonderful this is. You're so open and trusting. Unlike my wife. Sorry, ex-wife.

SHE SAID

"I feel a little uncomfortable holding your hand when there's a wedding ring on it."

BEST PART

He's got a daughter your age and you're sure to be great friends.

WORST PART

When his neighbor spotted him, he quickly pushed you under the table.

23. Creepy Non-Blinker

THE DATE

He's not like the other guys who could care less what you talk about. He listens to you, with intensity, like Hannibal Lecter listened to Clarice Starling.

HE SAID

"I like it how you pronounce my name. Say my name."

HE SAID

"I have a cat. She looks like you. I think she'd like your scent."

HE SAID

"You look great. I could just eat you . . . with some fava beans and a nice chianti. Ftftftftftftft. Just kidding. But I could."

BEST PART

He never took his eyes off of you. Never.

WORST PART

You now have to change your cell phone number and locks, just in case.

24. She Was Pregnant

THE DATE

On her online profile she checked off A Few Extra Pounds. Unfortunately, Third Trimester wasn't a category.

DRESS

A free-flowing peasant top, drawstring pants, and sandals to accommodate her swollen feet.

HE SAID

Nothing. Sometimes words are insufficient.

SHE SAID

"Want to feel him? Here, that's his foot."

BEST PART

D-cup.

WORST PART

She has twins at home.

25. The Dutchman

THE DATE

Ladies, bring your checkbook. It's actually not so much that he's a spendthrift as he's a great believer in equality. Fifty-fifty exactly.

THE COST

Whatever it is, it's split right down the middle.

HE SAID

"I'll pay by credit card if you give me cash. I love miles."

SHE SAID

"No, really, the cab is on me. You broke the bank with those carnations."

BEST PART

He springs for half-price Mondays at Mr. Sushi.

WORST PART

A.k.a. Mr. Food Poisoning.

26. Needs a Green Card

THE DATE

When Judy from the mailroom promised to set her up with a handsome, suave (Eastern) European, Melanie couldn't turn her down.

DRESS

Members Only.

HE SAID

"Hello. Marry me."

SHE SAID

"I could only marry for love. Or ten grand."

BEST PART

Listening to him spontaneously pledge allegiance to the flag.

WORST PART

He slipped an I-130 residency sponsor form in front of her as she was signing her credit card slip.

27. Cockfight

THE DATE

Two live roosters enter, only one leaves.

LOCATION

Iloilo, Philippines. Or an illegally soundproofed basement.

HE SAID

"You are really in for a treat. You have no idea what I had to do to get these seats."

SHE SAID

"What gets bloodstains out of clothes? Is it salt?"

BEST PART

The fights are quick. The roosters' legs have razors attached—one-rounders for sure.

WORST PART

He offers to buy what's left of the losing bird and roast it for dinner.

28. Cow Tipping

THE DATE

The wine and cheese picnic in a grassy meadow he promised wasn't what you had expected.

THE COST

$0. Like all the best things in life, or so he says.

HE SAID

"Come on now, you got to put your shoulder into it."

SHE SAID

"Wow. That cow seems to know you *really* well."

BEST PART

It's cheaper than cable.

WORST PART

Apparently, Farmer John doesn't take kindly to visitors. And he owns a double-barrel shotgun.

29. Was It a Date?

THE DATE

You have friends in common and even met up for lunch a couple times over the years. When he asked you out to a movie, the question was: Is it more of the same, or is he taking it to the next level?

DRESS

A mystery. The spaghetti strap tank is too suggestive, but a hooded sweatshirt makes you look like one of the gang.

HE SAID

"I couldn't decide between a romantic comedy and an action movie. So I hope this documentary is okay."

SHE SAID

"I find global warming so romantic."

BEST PART

There's an exciting tension all night long.

WORST PART

It goes completely unresolved. And his text the next day—"i had a great time. UR cool"—doesn't settle the issue.

30. Breakup

THE DATE

The last—short and sweet, or long and torturous, you can never tell.

LOCATION

Doing it over the phone is out of the question. A public place is best (so there are witnesses if she tries to stab you). Unfortunately, she chose the location of your first kiss. Looks like it's an all-nighter . . .

HE SAID

"I'll never love anyone the way I loved you." (Translation: *"Can I have your hot cousin Lisa's phone number?"*)

SHE SAID

"I hope we can still be friends." (Translation: *"I hate you."*)

BEST PART

Breakup sex.

WORST PART

You have to start going to the gym again.

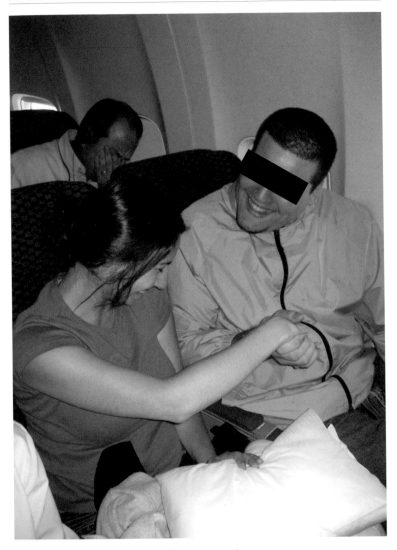

31. Airtroduced

THE DATE

The Los Angeles to New Zealand hump. What could have been a great time to finally read *Middlemarch* turns into a twelve-hour pickup attempt.

LOCATION

Sadly, coach.

HE SAID

"Man, I can't believe a babe like you would be traveling alone." *(That was his opening line. It only gets worse…)*

SHE SAID

"Tickle me under my blanket one more time and I will have you handcuffed by the air marshal."

BEST PART

It turns out he's allergic to peanuts.

WORST PART

He's on your return flight, too.

32. Reality Show

THE DATE

Two strangers get to know each other over a candlelight dinner. It sounds ideal—except for the crew members, the cameras, the klieg lights, and the fact that this is going to be nationally broadcast.

LOCATION

Fly bar. Then sound booth to overdub—the boom mic wasn't working.

HE SAID

"Hey, I think you're great. But I already do a stand-up routine about Irish girls. Do you have any cute Asian friends?"

SHE SAID

(*Crying to camera on her way home*) "Even though we only knew each other for twenty minutes, I never loved anyone like I loved him . . . This would be perfect material for a song. Did I mention I'm a singer? I have my own Web site . . ."

BEST PART

Free round-trip airfare to the set, free dinner, free fifteen minutes of fame.

WORST PART

Your hometown's economy was riding on you. You can kiss that homecoming parade goodbye.

33. Mechanical Bull
Riding Lawsuit

THE DATE

A moment on the steer, a lifetime in the Supreme Court of Alabama.

LOCATION

Cowboy Bar and Grill just off of I-85.

HE SAID

(*To his attorney*) "I swear I didn't see her do that fifth shot of Jägermeister."

SHE SAID

(*Just before being catapulted head-first to the ground*) "Look at me! No hands!"

BEST PART

Collecting thousands in disability insurance.

WORST PART

Getting dumped while you have a feeding tube in your mouth.

34. Xtreme Date

THE DATE

A new trend in alternative dating. Mountain biking, jogging, whitewater rafting, karate—these dates will certainly break the ice, if not a leg.

LOCATION

Class 5 rapids. Later, the emergency room.

HE SAID

"No, really, this is fine for a beginner."

SHE SAID

(*To herself*) "Cold. So cold. Must stay conscious . . ."

BEST PART

A break from the usual dinner and coffee date.

WORST PART

Six months in traction.

35. Lapdog Date

THE DATE

When she said her best friend was a dog you thought you could just pawn her off on your cousin. Little did you know you'd be watching her French-kiss an overgrown rat all night.

LOCATION

Miss Maple's Doggy Heaven. Everything on the menu is liver flavored.

HE SAID

"Is it really true a dog's mouth is cleaner than a human's?"

SHE SAID

"Little Bella really likes you! She usually *hates* men."

BEST PART

Her cuddling needs are taken care of.

WORST PART

Dating one bitch is bad enough.

36. Loud Bar

THE DATE

Your date looks cute. Too bad you can't hear a thing. For all you know, he doesn't even speak English.

LOCATION

A club with as many flashing, strobing lights as booming beats per second. A whole wall has been converted into a woofer.

SHE SAID

"Whaaaaaaat??!! Huhhhhh??!!"

HE SAID

You have no idea.

BEST PART

You don't have to worry about your comments being interesting, clever, witty, or tasteless.

WORST PART

It goes from blind date to deaf date quite rapidly.

37. Best Friend's Dad

THE DATE

After your best friend Kirsten slept with your boyfriend, you decide to enact the ultimate revenge.

LOCATION

Dinner and drinks: $80, on him. The look on Kirsten's face when she learns that you bedded the man who taught her how to roller-skate: Priceless.

HE SAID

"Are you sure Kirsten is okay with this? I think I just saw her in the parking lot slashing your tires."

SHE SAID

"I always thought you were really attractive, Mr. Adams. Remember when you helped me build that volcano diorama for the science fair?"

BEST PART

You can now suggest to Kirsten that she call you "Mommy."

WORST PART

He demands that you call him "Big Daddy."

38. One Night Stand

THE DATE

Usually occurs around closing time when the desperate spot each other across the bar.

DRESS

Less is more.

HE SAID

"My place or yours?"

SHE SAID

Just giggled while shoving him into the cab.

BEST PART

You are getting some!

WORST PART

You are getting some (crabs)!

39. Triple Indie Feature

THE DATE

When he asked if you wanted to go the movies, you were expecting a romantic comedy. Six hours of subtitles later, you can't wait to get home.

THE COST

Two movie tickets. He made you sneak into the other ones.

HE SAID

"I find dwarves so evocative, don't you?"

SHE SAID

"Wake me up when the dream sequence is over."

BEST PART

The previews, as always.

WORST PART

Getting deep venous thrombosis (DVT) from sitting still for six hours.

40. Bad Playdate

THE DATE

Gabriel's parents arranged for the infamous Johnson sisters to come over. Though roughly the same age as Gabriel, they each have a foot on him, which they leverage to their advantage—double noogies, headlocks, and tickle torture.

LOCATION

Playroom/torture chamber.

HE SAID

"No, no, no, no, no, no! Help! Somebody!"

SHE SAID

"What? You want to play dress-up? Sis, get the mascara, rouge, and that summer dress I saw hanging in the bathroom."

BEST PART

The video of the makeover places third in *The World's Craziest Home Movies.*

WORST PART

The bra fits.

41. She Didn't Shut Up

THE DATE

To avoid any awkward silence, she spews forth a run-on sentence comprised of commentary about her life so far, a recitation of the menu, her great ambitions, and the haunting traumas of her upper-middle-class family.

LOCATION

Unfortunately, a very quiet restaurant.

HE SAID

"Uh-huh. Yeah. You don't say. Hmm. Uh-huh."

SHE SAID

". . . which is when my parents got divorced which likely resulted in my older brother Jason dropping out of college to join an ashram where he got addicted to black tea and then got involved in an herbal products pyramid scheme which brings me back to my point that . . ."

BEST PART

The brief moment she choked on a carrot.

WORST PART

When the waiter knew the Heimlich maneuver.

42. Meet My Homies

THE DATE

A quiet evening at home suddenly turns into a night of Philly blunts, Hennessey, gin and juice, and his posse just "kickin' it."

LOCATION

Your crib.

SHE SAID

"Stop trying to get my cat high."

HE SAID

"Just keepin' it real, sistah."

BEST PART

Flashing gang signs at the neighbors.

WORST PART

Turns out your neighbors are Crips.

43. NASCAR/Secondhand Smoke

THE DATE

Lower-deck tickets to NASCAR, the most popular sporting event in America, featuring free emission fumes and noise pollution. But it's more than a sport; it's also a drinking game.

THE RIDE

He picks you up in his pride and joy—a modified 2007 Mitsubishi Eclipse with the licensed *The Fast and the Furious* conversion kit.

HE SAID

"I love the smell of exhaust in the morning!"

SHE SAID

"Wait, so I drink every time there's a yellow flag, and twice when there's a multicar wreck?"

BEST PART

It's much better than watching NASCAR on TV, where every other commercial is for erectile dysfunction.

WORST PART

Having to hear him say "hummina, hummina" every time the lone female driver passes the stretch of track closest to you.

44. Arrives in Pajamas

THE DATE

On the fifth date, he decided to take the relationship to the next step—the sleepover.

LOCATION

In the spirit of Hugh Hefner, he sported Brooks Brothers flannel PJs. A Victoria's Secret teddy was laid out for her.

HE SAID

"I just feel really comfortable around you."

SHE SAID

"I think I gave those pajamas to my dad for father's day."

BEST PART

What he lacked in underwear he made up for in flowers and champagne.

WORST PART

He started pitching a tent halfway through *Finding Nemo*.

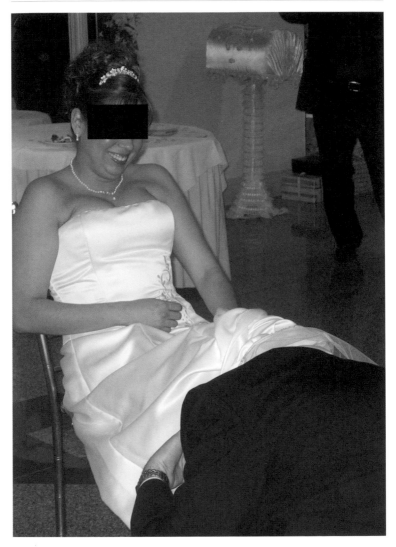

45. Wedding

THE DATE

You're the only single bridesmaid. You're going to look bad enough in that shrimp-bisque-colored dress—arriving solo would put you over the edge. Unfortunately, the only person you could find was your next-door neighbor, who will go anywhere if he can drink for free.

LOCATION

A three-hour boat cruise. Don't think you're getting out of this one easy.

HE SAID

"Cash bar?! Give me twenty bucks."

SHE SAID

(*To the father of the bride*) "We're still in the courtship phase."

BEST PART

He certainly livened things up by cutting in on the bride and groom's first dance.

WORST PART

When he dove under the bride's dress, beating the groom to the garter.

46. Date to Mate

THE DATE

When he suggested that your pedigree dogs meet, it sounded perfect. He's cute, and has breeding on the mind.

LOCATION

The dog park, where anything goes.

SHE SAID

"This is going to be great. Hybrids are all the rage."

HE SAID

"Are you sure this is going to work? Fifi looks awfully small."

BEST PART

Watching the action put a real spark in his eye.

WORST PART

Apparently, it didn't take. The next week, you saw him chatting up some tart with a Pekingese.

47. Dim Sum

THE DATE

You thought dim sum would show you were spontaneous and open to new things. Like intestine.

LOCATION

An authentic Chinatown dim sum hall: no menus, little English spoken, and inside every steaming bamboo bowl a mystery.

HE SAID

"Mmm. This sure smells good."

SHE SAID

"You just ate braised chicken foot."

BEST PART

Your fortune cookie said you might get lucky tonight.

WORST PART

Your stomach has different ideas.

48. Car Ran Out of Gas

THE DATE

It was supposed to be dinner and drinks. Instead it was gas cans and lots of walking.

LOCATION

Route 4 off the Pennsylvania Turnpike.

HE SAID

"You're not going to believe this but . . ."

SHE SAID

"Do you have any idea how much these shoes cost? Manolos, Bob. Man-o-los."

BEST PART

Walking together in the rain could be construed as kind of romantic.

WORST PART

Or it could be construed as a wet T-shirt contest.

49. Wicked Cheap

THE DATE

He said dinner and a movie, and technically he delivered. His and hers burgers and an action flick on the mini–DVD player Velcroed to the dashboard.

LOCATION

The drive-thru.

HE SAID

"I'd say go for it and supersize, but darn, they took it off the menu. Maybe the Hamburglar stole it? Hope Mayor McCheese doesn't put him in county McJail. Ha! But seriously, you're small. One cheeseburger should do it."

SHE SAID

"I'm a stage-four vegan."

BEST PART

You found Raisinettes in the glove compartment.

WORST PART

When the battery ran out on the DVD player and he suggested "creating our own entertainment."

50. Company Christmas Party

THE DATE

Until you had five cups of eggnog at the annual Xmas bash, you never realized how cute Allison from accounting was.

LOCATION

The festive twelfth-floor conference room.

HE SAID

"I promise it won't be weird on Monday."

SHE SAID

"Are you familiar with the current definition of sexual harassment in the workplace?"

BEST PART

She tells you what everybody makes.

WORST PART

Even Ezra in the mailroom makes more than you do.

51. Your Date

THE DATE

LOCATION

HE SAID

SHE SAID

BEST PART

WORST PART

Writing contributions by Daniel Berman and Lori Segal
Significant photography by David Berman
Publicists: Wendy Morris, Katie Rosin
Illustrations: Laurel Tyndale
Producer: Daniel Berman

THE PHOTOGRAPHED

Proposes on First Date: Ben Seay, Dorothy Cowan
Joe Hickey: Briana K. O'Connor, Cameron Smith
The Doodler: Tanya Choi
Karaoke: Courtesy of Robert Simmons, Mike Lunt
She Was in It for the Meal: Alan Corey, Janice DeVito
Surprise! You Were Related: Kerry Barker, Daniel Berman
Shorter in Person: Jeffrey C. Piermont
Spinach in Teeth: Amanda Ezell
Ménage à Blackberry: Deborah Lester
Hope You Like Meat: Sara Steenrod
Conjugal Visit: Mark Pennington
Passover: Marianna Racz, Mike Drootin
First Date: Lloyd A. Johnson Jr., from Don Bosco Tech High School
Too Hot: Ana Crisan
Dating the Bartender: Joe Ovbey, Sally Watson
AA Meeting: Sarah Hvass, Brian Berrebbi, Justin Purnell
Kiddy Date: Matt Stallworth, Alicia Curtis
Almost Divorced: courtesy of Rajesh Taneja, Urban Mixer
Creepy Non-Blinker: Joe Ovbey
She Was Pregnant: Bob and Sara Harty
Needs a Green Card: Matt Ohara
Cockfight: Malcolm Trevena
Was It a Date?: Colin Glaum, Nancy Shames
Breakup: Ana Arpa
Airtroduced: Lara Tal
Reality Show: David Berman, Jayson Atienza, Victoria Binzuger
Mechanical Bull Riding Lawsuit: Con Cutrer
Xtreme Date: Chris Bartle, courtesy of Clear Creek Rafting
Lapdog Date: Beth Joy Knutsen, Bella, Alan Corey
Loud Bar: Christian Coleman, Ryan Kominski
Best Friend's Dad: Harold Kramer, Molly Robertson
Triple Indie Feature: Lisa Ackerman
Bad Playdate: Gabriel, Savannah, and Brittany
She Didn't Shut Up: Jessica Smolins, Andrew Hannigan
Meet My Homies: Joshua Nagel and Zack Hirsch
NASCAR/Secondhand Smoke: Colin B. Heatlie
Arrives in Pajamas: Katie Druesdow, Joseph Graham
Car Ran Out of Gas: Matt Stanton, Jennifer Caldwell
Wicked Cheap: Nik Outchcunis

Company Christmas Party: Chris and Eva

THE PHOTOGRAPHERS

Proposes on First Date: Pat Williams
Joe Hickey: David Berman
Karaoke: Lisa Simmons
She Was in It for the Meal: Christian Coleman
Surprise! You Were Related: Christian Coleman
Shorter in Person: David Berman
Painfully Chivalrous: Darrell Taylor
Spinach in Teeth: David Berman
Ménage à Blackberry: David Berman
Hope You Like Meat: Sara Steenrod
Conjugal Visit: Mark Pennington
First Date: Courtesy of Lloyd A. Johnson Jr., from Don Bosco Tech High School
Too Hot: Ana Crisan
Dating the Bartender: David Berman, Scott Sanders
AA Meeting: Daniel Berman
Kiddy Date: David Berman
Almost Divorced: Rajesh Taneja
Creepy Non-Blinker: David Berman
She Was Pregnant: Bob and Sara Harty
Needs a Green Card: Matt Ohara
Cockfight: Malcolm Trevena
Cow Tipping: Renee Martin
Was It a Date?: Bill Cramer, Jake Jacobson
Breakup: Ana Arpa
Airtroduced: Julie Soefer
Reality Show: David Berman
Mechanical Bull Riding Lawsuit: Jon Cutrer
Xtreme Date: Courtesy of Clear Creek Rafting
Lapdog Date: Christian Coleman
Loud Bar: David Berman
Best Friend's Dad: David Berman
Triple Indie Feature: Daniel Buchbinde, Margot Leitman
Bad Playdate: Robert Johnson
She Didn't Shut Up: David Berman
Meet My Homies: Brian St. Cier
NASCAR/Secondhand Smoke: Colin B. Heatlie
Arrives in Pajamas: David Berman
Wedding: Jayson Atienza
Date to Mate: Mark Lorch
Car Ran Out of Gas: Stacey Bode
Wicked Cheap: Christine Brown
Company Christmas Party: Natalia Rode

ACKNOWLEDGMENTS

Thank you to everyone I met on JDate.com, AOL LOVE, and Craigslist's casual encounters. And I guess, to some, sorry; it was just research.

Everlasting gratitude to my agent Betsy Lerner. It's been ten years now since we met and every year it's getting better. Thank you for making my twenties.

The best for last: Bloomsbury. Colin Dickerman, Panio Gianopoulos, Karen Rinaldi, Alona Fryman, Yelena Gitlin, Suzie Lee, and Amy King; Beth Jordan and Jiyeon Dew in Bloomsbury's production department; Elizabeth Van Itallie, the cover designer who had the vision; and Tien Wah Press for bringing the job home.

To Bloomsbury's sales force, thank you for putting our little series beside—or on the same bookcase as—your top-shelf literary roster. For a book that's half photos, it's quite humbling, and awesome.

Also, I apologize. There were worse dates than these. But to maintain some essence of a PG-rating, I pared them down so the book could sell in Peoria, Illinois.

More thank-yous: Ellen Racz, Greg Racz, Alec Brownstein, Alexander Bain, Bob Arnold, Georg Wallner, The Jervi, Ryoko Yamada, Maciek Musia, Ryan Horn, Jared King, John Lensgraf, Scott Smith, Jeff Licht, Jared King, George Pollard, Julie German, Chris Hausbeck, Lena and Christian Candia, Natalia Sherman, Pete Williamson, Annie Cooper Angelino, John Lue, The Pope, Maya Newman, Caitlin from Virginia, Brandi, also from Virginia, Andy Smull, Emily Midorianna, Paul Armstrong, Rajesh Taneja, Howard Kwong, Briana K. O'Connor, Soon, Random Echo, Heather, Plastic Candy, Courtney Thompson, Clear Creek Rafting, Jolanta Musial, Bill Brelsford, Marciej Musial, David Roberts, Danli, Nic Bannon, Brooke Ellsworth, Jacqui Lane, Melissa Liebling-Goldberg, Jacob Waldman, Andrew Keil, Sarah Peveler, Bradley J. Lambert, The Experts: Mitch Bennett, Frank Peveler, Richard Hair, Kevin Jenkins, Simon and Farrah Gibbs, Scott Sanders, Brian Gadinsky, Tom Mazza, Lori Segal, Jethro Lieberman, Scott Studenberg, Mat Gordon, Alicia Curtis, Matt Stallworth, Tracey Redmond, Sarah Natochemny, Kirk Damato, Sarah Heiman, Brandon Rivera, Erin Anderson, Susan Surface, Jane Catflisch, Cameron Smith, Amanda Ezell, Alyssa Byrd, Harold Kramer, Molly Robertson, Seth Lieberman, Enzo Velazquez, Lauren Cofield, Nate Taylor, Vicki Lesiw, Bill Kramer, Clayton Hemmert, Craig Holzer, Sherri Margulles, Debbie McMurtrey, Fieldston professors: Sandra Cullinan, Bob Montera, Joe Algrant; Rolph Blythe, Irene Lacis, Andrew Nurnberg Agency, The Abner Stein Agency, CrewCuts, Kay Luo, Dave McClure, Anil Godhwani, Chesley Heymsfield, Stu Sternbach, Alex Finklestein, Stacey Soefer, Michelle Soefer, Dr. Soefer, Cindy Soefer, Ellie Francisco, Lucia Martinez Martinez, Jonathan Solari, Samantha, his girlfriend, Jeff Finkelstein, Esquire, Laura Mozes, Johnny V., Benjamin Watson, Chris Nichols, Amy Nichols, Katie Eckert, Kelly Brickner, Rosie DiMarzo, Lauren Goldberg, Ryan D'Agostino, Sara D'Agostino, Baby D'Agostino, Jason Tandon, Bill Noto, Scott Mitnick, Nicholas Apostolatos, Michelle Katz, Ben Coplon, Julie Rappaport, Josh Cahill, Daniel Racz, Rebekah Racz, Andrew Smith III, Dunow, Carlson & Lerner Lit Agency.